THE UNCERTAINTY PRINCIPLE

Bill Mayer

OMNIDAWN

RICHMOND, CALIFORNIA

2001

Also by Bill Mayer:
Longing

"The Celestial City" was published in *Scratchgravelhills* 1

"The Baffled" and "#18, America is an island" from the Greece Series were published in *Paris/Atlantic #1*

"The Visitors" was published in *Caterpillar 20*

"Reducing Planes" and "#10 I was tired of angry, tired of excuse" from the Greece Series was published in *Ironwood 17.*

"#1 The idea, he said, is to rescue them," "#16 These days I would see through the entire visible world," and an earlier version of "After" were published in *Ironwood 19.*

© Copyright Bill Mayer 2001
All rights reserved. No portion of this work may be reproduced or transmitted in any form or by any means, electronic or mechanical, including photocopying and recording, or by any information storage or retrieval system, without permission in writing from Omnidawn Publishing.

Book cover and interior design by Philip Krayna Design, Berkeley, California

Cover photograph by Bill Mayer: *Street in town of Paroikia, island of Paros, Greece*

O̶MNIDAWN™

Published by Omnidawn Publishing
Richmond, California
www.omnidawn.com
(800) 792-4957

ISBN: 1-890650-06-4 (paper)
9 8 7 6 5 4 3 2 1

⊛ Printed in the United States on recycled paper.

Contents

PART TWO : *Localities*

PART ONE

Greece

1

The idea, he said, *is to rescue them.*
I looked down the well.
Stone and marble masonry, handsomely done,
for maybe twenty-five or thirty feet.
Then, dimly, water, and insects breaking the surface.
It was hard to concentrate.
The heat rose in the field, taking all color away.
Soon we would be transparent, the stubble,
the two sad cows, and the well.
Who in hell cares about them? I said.
Dead, dead, dead. What difference does it make?
They lived their lives, well or not,
and that's that.
Go down the well, he said.
We stood there then, didn't move.
Into the evening. The late moon
made no difference. The wind was up all night,
and has continued. The fields, the cows, the dead,
all wait—there's no need to hurry.
Towards morning I said,
Look. No one pays me for this, nor even asks for more.
He spread his arms outward, palms up,
shaking. *Get down, Man!* he shouted.
And I got down.

2

The lapping water keeps them slightly apart.
The waves slap lightly, steadily,
against the boat. They sit, waiting
to bring in the hundred hook line,
and Venus is the brightest thing anywhere.
A slight haze haloes it.
They could touch one another,
but they don't. He starts to row.
The lights of other boats and other islands
shine, low on the water.
They cannot be sure which are moving.
     .   .   .

He lays his hand
on the rise of her buttocks.
She is not quite asleep.
Some distance is best, he thinks; not too close.
They wake frequently and know the other is awake
as well. Once, the darkness is filled
with the singing of a nightingale;
later, there is a cat fight. When dawn comes
they make love wordlessly.
He gets up then, heats water.
They listen to the birds together.

3

Up early. Into the Parian morning
half asleep to urinate. The Venetian tower
where the brothers killed their sister
before they went out to die
has no sunlight on it yet.
A turkey whimpers somewhere down the hill.
Will there be enough water in Summer?
And what about the scorpions? I worry.
How many years are left in which
I may call myself young, or fairly young?
I throw water down the hole, bring
the bucket back, fill it, set it on the porch.
I go in, start to make coffee.

4

At the farmhouse down the hill
where I go each morning for milk
and eggs, a child is crying.
Through the sound of the cicadas
that noise works on me like a rasp.
Soon it is me crying, unreasonable and surly
no matter how much the mother shouts
or pleads. I want to go down
and hit him, so the madness
that is pain will stop shrieking,
so there can be silence again
and I may turn my eyes outward
and see the real world, as always,
shining and implacable.

5

I am standing outside in the early morning
trying to clear my mind of the dream
about how it feels to be killed
in an air accident. When the priest appears,
he is walking carefully through the vineyard
with the owner and his family, preparing
to consecrate the chapel behind
where his parents are buried.
I go quickly inside. Then they ring the bell
and begin singing that rhythmic chant
the Orthodox Church uses.
The man is seventy-two, will be
buried here and his wife as well.
As I stand near the back kitchen window
listening, I can see the ground spinning,
the tiny houses,
and I try to hold on to something,
understanding clearly there is nothing,
nothing at all to hold.

6

The night comes as the beginning of the show
at the Planetarium in San Francisco.
I mean the way the Plane trees
grow so intensely black against the darkening
but brilliant sky. Closer to this island
than ever to the Southern California suburbs
I came out of, I wait, naked
under the stars, for the thin moon
to clear the stuccoed bedroom wall.
Jan reads on the old bridal bed inside.
I tell myself I'll go in to her
when the last bat flickers off to feed in the darkness,
but keep postponing the moment,
afraid the beauty out here cannot be matched.

7

He stands in the dry field, looking for shards.
The stony field is covered with them, rough,
the glaze weathered off. Water jars, he thinks,
because they are thick and near an old well
still used for the Summer herd of goats,
the islet's only inhabitants. The air is filmy
with a water haze; heat rises from the thistles.
Across the strait, Paros is a mirage, its soft gold
insubstantial, as though one could wave it away.
He sometimes kneels, scrapes at the dirt with his hands,
uncovers pieces that have set with the rocks so long
they cannot be separated without breaking. He discovers
nothing unusual, nothing fine. It is a perfect day.

8

I sit under the flowering pomegranate tree
by the stone water basin at midday;
reach down into the cool water
for a bottle of wine, thinking
of the librarian I knew
who hid in a tiny storeroom during lunch
to play his clavichord. A simple box
that could pass for a folded chessboard
until you opened it, and played,
and had to be completely still
to hear anything. An instrument
not meant for an audience, and he said
to me sadly: When Mozart was my age,
he'd been dead for two years.

9

I was half asleep in the hot shuttered room
when the phone started ringing.
Walked into the dining room slowly,
then the other bedroom. Confused,
hurried to the kitchen, even
opened the door out back.
The trees were cool and dark.
The cats came up, thinking to be fed.
But there is no phone I remembered,
a little frightened as it kept ringing.
There's nobody home, no one. Not yet.

10

I was tired of angry, tired of excuse.
I sat outside while the dark took the trees
like black flame, with blue brightness behind.
The wind stopped and the night birds paused.
No singing, no bells, the night shuddered sideways.
The farmers say you cannot sleep under the olive,
you cannot breathe in its shadow.
It is death and madness. Yes, and the old woman too,
who sits on the stones, propped against the wall,
unable to raise her hand for help. Black on white.
I light a candle. The anger is still there,
crouching in a corner. It freezes,
and we stare at each other, fascinated.
Here, I say, take me then,
not like a penitent, but as one who finds
the habit of living an urgent thing.
And then I tell myself: Don't waste me.

11

Alba

Just before dawn I go out
to watch the bats return
to the hole behind the shutters
of our house.

12

Out picking plums,
trying to avoid the large spiders
that wait between the branches,
thinking that what I want to learn
no one cares about. Hating
the arcane but being pushed there.
I brush against a web
and watch one scurry to a branch
and wait. I take the hot plums
and get back to the porch.
Look down at my body to make sure
and then lie in the sun.
If I shake the web again, I wonder,
will the message get through?

13

He dreams of haze, tells me
the world is most wonderful when dimly seen.
He is adamant, says
that photography is a mistake of perception.
Our earth, he claims, is what Kirschner saw
in the late pictures, not Adams.
We sit out on the porch in the hot August morning.
I have shown him already how the north and west
windows are filmed with salt. Which pleased him.
Together we watch clouds form over Profitas Elias,
and then blow away. He is a danger,
approving of qualities which promote imprecision.
We have gone over this for years,
but under different guises. As a boy,
I remember he hated science, but that, of course,
he has amended. His argument, as we drink our thick coffee,
is subtler now. Truth by aphorism.
Gods decorate his speech, and you can almost see them
when he tells of shadows in the trees,
a darkness over the stream.
Under a stone anything may be waiting.
I consider my plain world and partnership
with the other animals. For me, the seasons shift,
the thistles merely dry. Yesterday, for instance,
while walking up the hillside,
I found a spring, now unused, and ancient cistern
below it. The crack went back twenty feet

that I could see, deep into the mountain.

I stared for a long time.

The bamboo and mulberry wavered in the evening breeze.

Precision is change, I thought.

I'd better find a different kind of magic.

And not tell him.

14

Again I go to the tower
to ask the murdered sister what it was like.
Were they tender? Did any of them cry?
Or were they simply stern, blinded by their idea
of honor? One can believe anything.
I climb up and call to her:
Think what the Algerians would have done;
it makes a difference.
But she does not answer.
The wind beats at the stone, finally
forcing me down. Those brothers took their deaths
like candy, away, far from this place.

15

The man looks English, say, mid nineteenth century,
the sort of man Cameron photographed. When we meet
he always says: *We're not done here yet, are we?*
Which is not encouraging. When then I tell him dreams,
he is not amused, is even skeptical of my intent.
This afternoon he came out of the back room
saying: *Intelligence is our only enemy.*
It shows us what we lack and can never get.
He was furious. Great, I thought. Come to Greece
and instead of gods
you get some scowling Dr. Arnold figure,
a Victorian moralist who sounds at times
like the Rimbaud you detest. Now he's in the other room
muttering insults. Somewhat unsteadily, I get up, go outside.
He doesn't speak, or even look up.
I smile to myself, think I must be the only man
on this island who fights with the dead.
I touch the ripening olives, then pick a fig, eat it,
and go down to the toilet. When I get back,
the two kittens come up. They're getting older now,
and one is frail. The three of us sit on the porch
and consider. I notice the north wind is starting up again.
I should treat it as a sign.
But what comes next, I wonder, where do we go from here?

16

These days I would see through the entire visible world,
across the stony fields, past the small grove of olive
in the fold of the valley to the gold mountain, and beyond,
into a sky filled with blue dust. These days
it is not just Greece, or the flowering thistle,
or the smell of thyme; not even the drying donkey shit on
    the track,
or the hawk cries of farmers calling across the fields.
All the wind and sun lead elsewhere
and I cannot stop as I walk over the mountain
towards town to buy groceries, nor know what use
these stones have of me, if any.
The gods and their stories seem insubstantial,
as though they figured temporarily in some more rigorous
    purpose.
They evolve into the landscape along with the rock walls
and the fat lizards that drowse on their warmth.
My body hurries along under a pressure of not knowing.
I call out, not caring what might answer,
but believe something will, and am prepared.

17

I run the way all run, I bob and weave.
I spend half my days
planning to avoid
doing what I must. I am anyone.
On the Greek bus we squeeze each other so
no one knows how it is done.
I move so fast I am the machine
that won't stop.
It goes on and on. These days
I open the door expecting
who knows what. The shutters creak
and slam in the wind. It's not
the wind telling me, it's he
who hurries, who knows how asleep I am.
I cannot wake for moving. I run.
I run.

18

America is an island. Floats in the blue haze
just south of Andiparos. I can't see it
from my window but know it's there
all right. When the owls have quieted
late at night, I wake
to hear it singing sweetly. Of promise,
and the familiar. I go out to the porch.
Under a waning moon the night ferry takes back
all those I love. Small, bright bulbs on a string.
Above the sound of the engine there is laughter,
and what I imagine to be good conversation.
But the little island of America fades in the new dawn.
How much I love and detest it. How often I have said
to the world: this is not me, this is me.

19

Cover your tracks are the last words
I hear before the dream dissolves,
like powder in water. Fine, I think,
but what will I want tomorrow?
Will I have gained anything worth keeping?
It is late Summer. There are shots
down in the valley. The Greeks walk slowly
through the fields, shooting the tiny finches.
I remember as a child waking early,
looking through the black trees
to the red morning brightness, sick
with fear and excitement. It's the same now.
I must be leaving for darkness
in the warmth and ripeness of the year.

20

Our life was easy.
We lacked nothing. Lived here,
learned. We spent our time
with one desire: to say the simplest things
to each other, without guile.
But this was not easy at all.
I tell you, our life was hard.
So sweet and painful this island was,
soft on the Aegean.
The ships passed by.
We lay on the bed pretending.
We were lonely, finally.
Sad. Circled each other
with caution. We left nothing.

PART TWO

Localities

Reducing Planes

1

Trees. Snow. Trees further away.
In the gray light, they are as pasted on a board,
the snow merely empty white, the further away
just smaller trees. This is theory.

2

I go out to the white fields pretending
not to be human. Then stop, wonder what it is
I attempt, or mimic. I flounder in the snow,
falling through the crust.
The spirit beyond human doesn't carry much interest.
There is choice here: a god whose skin shines,
or a hollow in a bank.

3

It is not a matter of cruelty; just that,
swinging his arms, he knocks the man down.
He does not even notice until after.
Then he grieves.

4

In the darkness he burns snow into the photograph.
Too much light will make it drab; too little
and it remains empty. He works until late,
changing papers, exposures, chemicals,
going over it again and again.

Archaeologist

China. The great burial mound must have treasures
    beyond imagining.
Maybe not, but anyway we decide to leave,
let the Commune continue plowing as it has done for
    however long,
pack our tools and be off.
It would be better to dig in the sea.
It would be better not to dig at all. I think
it would be far better to dream of digging, while earth parted
and out they came, damp-odored, courteous,
their sweet, clay hands touching our faces to reassure, lead,
perhaps even, uncover, us.

The Baffled

I look out the window to the radio tower lights.
A reflection of myself gets in the way.
The skin and hair attract me, transparent against the black,
staving off darkness, still a part of it.
Which must be what dying is: a slow, dark
sucking out of what we see in the glass.
As when the nurse bends over, mouth moving but without
    sound.
Like that, I'd guess, even the white sheets going dim,
the familiar in retreat, becoming strange.

As a child on the narrow bed, I lay watching the tiny, red bulb
in the hallway that showed the furnace was working.
I did not think, or pray;
just held on, too afraid to tell them I was afraid.

Now my grandmother is giving up her arms, her legs.
She takes nothing as she peels them off,
but it's not as though she were asking. Not a trade.
It hurts to move so she moves less.
When I phoned, she didn't want to talk; she was beyond that.
Good-bye. Good-bye. The letters we send go into the night.

The Garden

In our light the world is unmade.
The crabapple tree blossoms and the ferns
below it send out their fragile heads.
The cats move in the leaves. They curl, half hidden,
watching as awkwardly we make our home.
We try to make our home
but are unhappy. The grosbeaks call
in the gray dawn. If they could wake us then
or if we could wake. In the pines the sounds passes.
It is difficult to hear, difficult to wake
as we stutter and do disservice to the little space
we have. It is a world unmade, a reiteration
of leaves, making and forgetting, waking
in the newly silent nights, our eyes watering
as though glass had lodged under the lids in sleep.
The pain that blooms and its odor
is part of our garden, perhaps, at times, lovely,
where no one comes—in these narrow articulations.

The Visitors

The man's arm rests on my shoulder,
heavy on me as we walk.
I am getting advice. Always, on these walks,
I go with a teacher.

Am I attractive? Will I be loved?
The man is confident, but not,
I sense, for me. His confidence
is his own affair.

The clouds are stuffing the sky.
Will he try to seduce me?
I wonder vaguely, looking up.

We walk
as though we were waiting.
The shops pass us by
with the doors swinging.
A waiter would like us to try
his soup. On the lake
I count six different shades
of blue. What about the sky?
Or the mountains around the lake?
It is too bewildering.

Too unreasonable. Like holding back
an erection, modeling
for a woman I
cannot have.

Magic at an unimaginable cost.
A disordered life with condiments.

At the Hospital

The doors jerk open
and a gray man is wheeled
down the hall, one policeman thumping him
hard. I run after.
At the third floor, I get out
and look for the girl whose heart
is infected. Just beyond is the room
where my father waits for the drill.
But I hurry on. The ping-pong players
in the lounge don't notice.
A man grabs my arm. *Look, look,*
he says, pulling me into the room.
I stumble over the tubes and follow.
He points to the window and the sun
setting in our faces, filling the room
with red light. He closes the door
and the sound of the freeway rises
like an ocean. *I don't want
to die here*, the man wails. Christ
no, I think, shaking free; no.

Solitaire

Good. he said. Another loss.
Even the time spent wasting time
can be profitable. Like sickness.
The seconds leak out
like water from the mud dams
he built as a child.
It goes through his fingers
and down the slope. Hurry. Hurry.

This may clear out the junk.
Confused, he separates his life
into two piles;
as though he could get rid of
the extraneous, and take the shining,
the clear, hold it up to the world
and say: this is me. No other.

Song

Responsibility is a savagery.
But my employers insist and
we vacillate together,
counting, counting, to prove
I may move usefully
through the world.

The Excesses

Spending the day, all day, trying to begin.
Looking for gods in the room,
knowing they were near but
needing them now, this overcast day,
recovering from a cold,
with no money, thinking about baseball.
Believing. Working.
Trying to get ready.
Wanting to be a decent host.

#7, Summer

I am at my desk writing,
hear her bare feet, know
there's a towel wrapped
over her wet hair.
She pretends quiet
but wants attention.
I look up,
not smiling,
not pleased in any way
about her.

#31

She smoked. Sat on the bed
staring at me, afraid, her wide lips
pulling at the cigarette
while the other man waited for me to leave.
I couldn't love then,
asked for pain instead;
got it.

The Next Day, Still Waiting

All night awake
wanting her
while she slept with my friend.
And I with no rights
other than desire,
masturbating twice, an animal
out of sorts.
How little the gods tolerate
the domestic.

Wrong

There was only the gas station, a house,
and old, broken cars. The valley,
salt white in the center, bitterbrush
and creosote bush, the blank sky and sun.

I thought, driving fast,
the quiet would be enough. I'd arrive
at the emptiness of the heart
where salt glare hurt and pain cleaned,
and find nothing of value.

The Intimate

I bent down
so that the tree
looked like it was about to fall
off the edge of the hill. There,
I thought, was the place to build.
A house just strong enough
to stand while I lived,
a thing to be torn down after.
Odd to reach out
when no one's there.
But will be there. At least,
that is how I figure.

Allegiances

Pressed against the window, I could see them
along the low hills, the commune villages
marking where we were. Clos Vougeot, the hill
of Corton, Beaune of course, and further south
what must have been Meursault. The train rocked on
towards Avignon. The man with the packaged sandwiches
struggled by. In the dull November light,
that narrow strip of earth
was just another place to grow grapes.
I sat down again in the compartment.
The Italian was asleep, his snores letting
the rest of us smile to each other,
hesitantly, animals protecting our strangeness.

2 A.M.

My Lady sleeps, half-dressed,
her book still near her.
How much we read.
It's unhealthy,
a turning away, a dance
that lessens dancing.

After Separation

One day, the people in whose house we are staying
go away. Left alone, we are like adolescents,
embarrassed in the many rooms
filled with only us.
How lovely she is dressing up for me,
her nipples dark under a white blouse.
The past is like a door slamming
over and over. How shyly,
vulnerable as never before,
we make our approaches.

A Kind of Love Poem

for Linda

After our sad lovemaking I think of you,
wondering where you are but not really caring.
After desire, after the daily struggle
we work through, I can turn,
if to anyone, to you.
Or rather, it is you who appear.
I know I'm still a novice. But then,
the horrid self is my meat;
so courtesy, or kindness, or whatever
I think to give is a partial gesture.
But I love you nonetheless.
You are voiceless but present. I hear
from others things you say about me.
I gather my little information.
Oh lover I am, squeezing your hand, embarrassed,
my eyes at your ear or hair.
I am courtly, know my distances.
I meet the goddess.

The Quiet

On an impulse, you read me the letter
to your friend telling her
about us. Not that you planned it so,
but we are frightened seeing ourselves
as characters while some third voice
narrates. How impossible
it is to speak plainly.
I think of Tolstoy and his wife
arguing in the single diary
they both kept. Accusations, threats,
entreaties, but never a word
outside that book.

The Primitive

Her face is blank, a mask over nothingness
that permits itself to be made human by me.
She lets my moist breath brighten her,
becoming animate, and woman.
She allows, but I must yield
her encirclement of my busy world:
my red, my trees, my sweet numbers,
my warm, hungering flesh.
She gives me an interval.
For now, she lets me be.

Instructions

In the pool, you kept veering
to the side, but the instructor
pushed you back, deeper.
It has been years since you last remembered.
Start there,

in the desert outside of Hermosillo.
Take the road west to the coast. There,
are gold coins at Kino. Under the tent
in week-long rain.

That night the rain was warm.
Down the dark alley tangerine trees,
back fences, garbage cans, and the quiet houses.
The street lamps flickered.

As we crossed the river, the clanging
of the train went hollow. Space taking us,
and a blue night bulb. Where?
you ask. Where graves are built above earth.
I have no philosophy, you said,

But I burn oh yes. The oxygen starts red
and then blue. It's the cone of night
at the center. Start there, where there is no music.

Planet X

If, among photographs of countless stars,
if, comparing two plates of the same region,
the same stars, on successive nights, blinking
over sets of photographs, each square inch section
studied when the prints were still wet from the bath,
if, after months of labor, a star was seen to jump,
a tiny, inconsequential dot of light,
beyond all question neither comet nor meteor,
nor irregularity on the photographic paper,
could it then be said
we have discovered an island perhaps,
where the lotus grows or love flourishes;
may we at least look towards this speck
among the other specks of light upon a sea of black,
which is space, and see our own reflection,
which is the sun's, looking back, as though the gods,
innumerable, expanding, should turn for a moment,
shining vaguely still, to our eyes, and bless us?

Vermont, February

I went to the door
just in case
in the cold night there might be need,
or hunger, or even contact.
I stood, counting Jupiter and Mars,
translating the bright dots I saw
into the banded bodies I knew
from photographs. You have to do this
because a star is just a blob of light
getting larger and larger, but without feature.
The wind came over the snow.
I waited,
determined this time
not to go back.

The Celestial City

1

I walk the cinder path, looking for paradise
on this shore or else in whatever apartment
I might rent. In Los Angeles,
my room had three windows open to the air.
In the hot Summers, the birch trees
made a small, insect sound.
I'd follow. It led out past the suburbs,
to Djerba sometimes, or Isfahan.

2

We drive up the dark freeway
toward the pass and basin beyond.
It is Winter. Soon
I downshift into third.
In starlight, like a faint cloud, snow
reflected from the great city
on the other side. The engine
gets noisy as it strains up these mountains.
I am coming home, in spite of myself.

3

From a turnout on the ridge
you could look down over both sides,
the city on one, and on the other
the Mohave. The radio

picked up the station clearly.
Snow everywhere, and then Vivaldi,
his Venice, this air,
my small, black car shining in the whiteness.

4

When I heard them start the waltz,
I ran down to the shore with my water bottle.
I wanted to find a place so I could see the dancers.
Evolution Lake, an almost treeless basin,
with the great Darwin group behind.
The waltz floated out over the water,
that touching, just audible pause before the stressed,
second beat. I stood, in shorts and boots,
in the warm afternoon, held by the music,
the high, red collars and medals,
the silk shimmering as they turned.
Holding the plastic bottle, I watched them
and the orchestra as it played.
I could just see the Emperor, helmet
in his gloved hands, though the dancers
mainly obscured him. It was amazing.
Somehow the Court had survived, and they still danced
in chandeliered light. But it was time to start dinner,
and I wanted onions from the stream.
I got the water and started back.

All Day in the Sun

We are accidental. Haphazard.
The pitying gods sometimes notice us
but can do nothing. We clamor,
closing ourselves off, losing the little we have.
We shut out even fear
as though we had a home,
a television, blue and friendly.

The gods invent.
We see them, barely,
white petals against a hot sky.
We invent each other after their manner,
entering, trying to love,
thinking to present ourselves shyly,
just off the pavement, for their approval.

But they can't see us that way.
Nor would they care. The death inside us
is always growing, making us want so badly
we must hold ourselves and turn away.
Ah yes they pity but, perfect,
they accept only light, sometimes
a textured sheen.
Always a brilliance unknowable.

Leaving Again

She is hungry, pleads with him to want directly,
not to always imply. She says
she is growing old, but he is not interested.
She dries her hair over the gas heater,
brushes it. Blood from her shaved leg
stains the white pants.

Courtesy is not enough.
As the laughter goes on downstairs,
she is crying on the bed, too afraid even
to go down and face those people on the way to the bathroom.

What can be told when everything clots?
as he stands up and sits down, reaches for the blankets,
squeezes and lets go, walks to the other room,
sits down, comes back. Tell me she says. He can't.

Now they are getting ready to go again.
They have torn up their lives. For him
it is easy, for her it promises nothing.
They get in the car.

PART THREE

Entering a Dark Wood

Andiparos

While we waited for the boat to return
I went back into the cave. Boys were playing there
and I could hear their shouts echoing.
At the first room I turned on the flashlight.
Here was the mud fort where we smoked cigarettes
I had taken from my parents. A stairway
led to the left, and the children kept calling,
their voices more distant. I should have to hurry
or lose them for good. I went down
to the next level, then paused again,
looked at the walls, read the scribbled messages
from all those years: black walnuts, poison oak,
the older boy I cried at from the Dutch door
in fury while he laughed, and waved,
kindly I now think, and my parents took me in.
I wanted to stay, even go down further;
the dead re-appear, telling us
here is a place to rest, renew acquaintance,
sit down to eggs and bacon and all
we thought we had lost. I switched off the light.
I could hear the dripping of water somewhere nearby,
but no voices. I knew Jan must be waiting impatiently above,
wondering what I was up to now.
There is never a choice really: you go looking
for Byron's signature and find early North Hollywood.
She will wait. I must wait. The wind came up from below
cool and dank, as though it had some answer.

After

I no longer remember the daily clarity
of living in Greece, except that it was clear.
But what, for instance, did we talk about
those warm evenings when the sun slipped
behind the plane trees and we began to prepare dinner?
And later, when there was little to read and we were left
to each other in the high ceilinged rooms;
that must be where we failed.
I do remember the silence.
It would have taken more courage than we had to resist it.
But to have made a kind of music, not once,
not just at the beginning—how much clarity,
how much perseverance would it have taken?

How the Hardy Boys Can Help You

1

Not thinking. I opened the flap
and saw that picture:
the boy in the tree
peering with binoculars through the leaves
across the page where men were loading boxes
on trucks. Smuggling, probably.
Illegal, anyway. One man had a rifle.
It meant adventure.
Which brought me to the attic room,
the overgrown property next door
that seemed to me a jungle. In short,
aspects of that person long ago
I thought I had transformed.

2

The boy turns in his tree, pushes back
his cap, and grins. Since I am called, I go.
In the cove, in the damp, pre-dawn air,
we wait for the muffled sound of motorboats.
I want to tell him these lawbreakers are of no account.
Just children playing games.
Let this vigil be for better things.
He looks back at me, almost smiling in the dark.
Clearly, he knows something I do not.
Ssh, he says. Someone's coming.

The man has not changed,
he has merely grown older.
The children he has, the wife,
the authority he assumes, even
the demeanor he affects, all,
all break down. Have you come so far,
I wonder, to do so little?

3

These voices rarely subside. A clutter of half ideas,
temptations, defenses and cries.
Each breath a word, saying:
Confusion is best—with pools of clarity between.
Like in the southern ocean, an horizon filled with clouds,
but clear sky a small circle directly above.
The illusion one moves in a charmed space
though we know the clouds are spread evenly.

Granted happiness is unexpected, almost incidental.
I stop at the market, run through the rain
to buy milk. Say a few, friendly words
to the woman at the register, get back in the car
and watch the windows fog up.
Oh so happy I could dance.

But there's no use in fear, he says.
We've been up all night playing poker
while it snowed steadily. The lake has turned metal
and the pines black and white.
All night in the heated house.
In the morning, surprised, I count winnings
of about four dollars. Still the smiling man persists.
Fear is destructive, old evolutionary habit
no longer needed. How confident and smiling and sweet
he is. I struggle through the new snow
as close as I dare get to the lake.
A snowball fight would be better.
But they think they are being serious,
so I go back, try to read *Lear* to prove I am,
and fall asleep.

4

They are reckless today.
You can hear them
making love, and laughing.
Parfaits. All day listening
with envy in the dark room
to the two other floors
while the sun sang
of the south, while
angelfish darted.
What to hide from? What
law dare not break?

But the boy is impatient.
He is down, over the rocks,
and at the entrance.
You can still see the pale reflection
from the other men's flashlights.
Come on, he whispers, stage style.
It's a trap, I think. I know this book.
And what about the rescue? What about the fight?
Is my courage failing me, or do I want something better?
I stand up, bow stiffly, then close the covers.

5

The rain has stopped, at least for a little while.
Drops hang from the tips of the Japanese Maple.
The voices are quiet enough for me to hear
the cat purring and a distant plane.
Jan is asleep after our morning walk in the rain.
I go to the door and look out.
I will wake her. Then,
if she is willing, we'll follow them.

An Invocation

There was a man watching women
with shopping carts go to their cars
and unload toys. He put his finger
on the rust and rubbed, watched
warm air rise from the engines.
The man fancied himself with white collar
and steel glasses. He was glad.
Take away the god, linen, and the smell
of England. Give him instead
scorched rubber. Make her come back
without children or Christmas.
Oh, impossible.

Red Peak Dialectic

I worked up the face slowly, over loose rock
and scree. My badly blistered heels
started to bleed. Decided to pretend
I had no feet. Then concentrate on breathing,
or using my hands, or the view, which was fine.
At the summit, I arranged my lunch,
sat by the cairn, looked over the snowy basin.
In that story by Kerouac, it is all Buddha,
Buddha, when he and Snyder climb their mountain.
Is it wrong, I wondered, to be in love
with my own body, and the small amount
of pain it took to get here? I was lonely,
had been in the Sierra two days
and did not find it easy. Worried about the night,
and animals, and god knows what.
It's the same old void, Snyder says.
No thanks, I muttered, took my Western mind
and body down, carefully, with Petrarch
but without apologies later, hobbled into camp,
made dinner. Later, in the sleeping bag,
my feet throbbing, watched the great wheel of stars.

Southern California Prayer, 1956

Dear God, he said, age eleven,
Send over a 'Constellation' soon, low and loud,
to prove you exist,
to prove there is no death, that it's only,
as my grandmother says, an exchange
of bodies, new car for a used,
just once, today. If not, he thought
as eucalyptus blew under Santa Ana, later,
maybe tomorrow? I'll even cheat a little,
and keep my eyes open for a sign. Anytime.

The Way Home

In the shower he smelled chlorine.
Which brought back Southern California
and the attendant nightmare life he thought
he had got over. But what can one do
about childhood? His hair dyed slightly green
at its edges. Impossible to deny,
or even make up for, later.
Oh, he's been at it all right,
inventing the Sierra, Provence, Vienna, Greece, etc.
But those suburban neighborhoods, airplanes
he counted as they landed and took off
across the Valley, the swimming pools
and all the rest: ah, Van Nuys, Sherman Oaks,
North Hollywood; they will always come first.

Conscientious Objector

I feel a dull but persistent ache
in the joint of my right foot, and think
how lucky I am to have suffered,
unlike so many of my friends, such minor
physical pain. Decay seems so ingenious,
getting in unasked, refusing to leave.

At the Draft Board, years ago,
a friend's father, who volunteered to testify
on my behalf, asked if there was anything wrong
with me. Any little thing, he said, trying to help,
that could be the kernel of your future death.

First Love

In the liquor store at Hilo, I found
a ten year old Premier Cru Chablis.
It was cheap, so I bought two, just in case.
One was gone, the other a little dark, but still good.

Today we swam naked among Parrot Fish
and Tangs, afterwards got fish
in the Japanese town. It was hot,
bare feet in muddied grass.
It rained, pounding the tin roof
so that we couldn't talk, then stopped,
then rained again. The geckos barked
and raced over the screens to catch
insects. We drank the wine slowly,
with grilled opelu and mangos,
thinking of our culture, Europe,
in this alien land.

Strip Poker

I was walking in an oak-ringed, grassy field.
An old woman stumped up angrily.
You fake. she said. *Sympathy?*
You'll get none. She walked away, vibrating.

This is some way to begin, I thought,
without a chance to argue or defend.
Sit down, a voice said softly, from behind.
We have some business together.

Clearly this man had come to trade.
You take religion, I said, thinking to exploit
my own disadvantages. I can get along. He smiled.
Fine, fine. No visions, then. No magic.

As the sun wheeled higher and the Red
Tail's shadow went by, we talked. I knew
I should have to lose, give each precious gain
to this smiling, dark suited man.

The fields throbbed white, wavering
in hot summer air. Dark, dusky green
of the oak canyons. How could he be
so at ease? *Love,* he said.

All things then, he could have them all.
As though there were choices now.
He'd not leave me again, I knew.
But for form's sake, I'd protest,

press for lesser things. White field,
fake and all. A patient man
with the wind at his tie. *You keep Death.*
Behind the eyes it began to burn.

Cribbed From, And For, Lawrence Durrell

He held the shaving brush up high—
like a torch. Well, no. Rather like a rapier. And then
adroitly thrust home at the face in the mirror
in the manner of Rostand.
                Though that
did not make her come. They say herein
lies some consolation. This time
it led into the yard, into sage and ginesta,
where it stopped. White caps down the hill.
So the wind was up. It must have been
tomorrow.
                Or never. And the woman he loved?
Or refused to love? What was the difference?
Clean, wet hair and shaven, he stared
at the sour reflection. It would suffice.
These shadows were a life.

Childe Ballade

Tony said once you couldn't lie
in a group; someone would catch you out.
But couples could, and did, to each other,
and should never be trusted.

Or: You did this by bending over backwards
slowly, so far that fear took over
the body. Fear as a thing, like pulled muscle.
Now! shouted the therapist, to prove a point.
And yes, it's true. You sweat with it. Then

get you a silver dagger, and a graveyard,
and a moon, and, what else?
So they'd submit to it, week after week,
the new lover he'd met there also, talking, crying,
until she'd had enough. Let love go home. Or away.
No song, no song he knew fit.
He lived alone, then.

Der Rosenkavalier

How did the backs of my hands become puckered
and creased without my noticing?
Did it happen while they lay quietly
above the covers? Who is doing this?
And why does he let me watch it happen
with such clear senses?
They are dry, so I oil them repeatedly.
It sounds better to say they are weathered,
or tanned. I make a fist to smooth the skin.
But the fist has nothing to hit.

The Best Time

In the dark wood you are overweight.
You believe happiness and the good life
are not only possible, but well worth having.
You forget the confused desires you had
and look on the world with benevolence.
In the dark wood gods have so deserted you
you speak of them casually as old friends.
You really think there is a way through.
This hell is habit,
makes death seem rather comforting:
deep, deep in the ice where no one
feels anything, because they betrayed themselves.

Canto 34

The stars are just visible through the steadily widening hole.
If you go away, what is yours? Memory, of course,
and desire. Those are easy. The hunger for both
is not exactly tiring, but there is nothing to hold
once you arrive. Even the memory of Jan's body
kept alive by pain. Preferred, and without myth. I look up
to a pale sky just before dawn. I doubt I am ready.

Silences

The bright sun fills my room
as though light could caress.
It melts the ice crystals on the windows.
I see again the dirty March snow, the three
thousand miles, the loneliness.
I lie in bed in this beautiful white room
and listen to the clicking of the electric
blanket. I try to think, then try not to.
I have been careful too long.
Blame. Blame when there is none.
Only failure, and need.

Alto Rhapsody

She lies back and lets him make love to her.
It must be difficult because she is sad.
But she touches his body and gives herself to him.
She needs this. She has viewed her own body so often
in the mirror and has thought herself becoming old,
unable to love or be loved anymore. His excitement moves her.
The man she betrays by being here cannot understand
    this need,
or accept it. But she must feel whole again, or try,
and give herself to this troubled man who wants, and
    would love,
and touches her small breasts as though they were not
    quite tame.
Perhaps tonight he will not respond to her hand, nor
    her tongue.
He lies back after the effort, grateful anyway,
and she accepts that. He moves his hand along her
    lower belly,
caressing the long scar, making her young again.
She knows that the man she loves dies a little each time,
and that their love will die, but what other choice is there?
What is she to do? And that man is in shadow now, far away,
while this man is here, his body white and unprotected.
Later he comes inside her and she is quiet. They sleep.
Somewhere, in the keen air of winter, the third man weeps.

The Man Who Finished Feeling

After she left him, he thought he still had a gift.
He took a small but well-sharpened knife.
Delicately, he peeled back the skin, then the muscles.
He could then see, by looking at the mirror,
his own heart beating.
That's how he knew.

Schubert's Definition

So I take off the record, open the door
and listen. I am surprised that nothing I hear
implies happiness. I wonder, go outside
and water the plants on my little deck.
The March sun is warm but the air is not.
All this morning spent restless and guarded,
looking for a way out of sadness. I can feel
a gear shifting, some machine lurching into motion.
I touch the air, the sound. The city
I peopled never was, or could be.
I want to praise, and cannot.
I want sorrow to be translucent and bright.
I want, I want, said the child, and believed
that wanting could bring her back whole
and unmarked, without the clutter
of a single betrayal, without the responsibility
we all have for killing the thing we love.

New England

After days of steady rain, the clouds
start breaking up. I walk along North Street
carrying a small bag of fish.

The two people fighting across the street
are not holding much back.
Her voice is hard, loud and hurt,
his too soft for me to hear exactly what he says.
There could be menace in it, or just someone
trying to placate.
I wonder what she thinks he has done.

They are inside one of the apartments
of a large old building that faces the street
for half a block.
The windows are open
to let in the warm Spring air. Then
she almost screams: Get out! Get out!
I'm calling the cops!

I walk on, my heart taut,
feeling the unexpected heat on my neck.

Well Above Timberline

On the third day, I picked my way over talus.
Rain made the stones slick
and I was busy talking, talking, having
to talk when my eyes went bad,
having to keep it up because
they had only air and mouth
to hold me, only that rich loneliness
for my feet to grip. Stone ice
and blue, I was the gulping fish of fear;
I couldn't focus, couldn't cry.
The naked man had quitted me.
I bled; my knees were tired from the pounding.
But the great stone field sloped down,
sloped down and further out of sight.
Not having to do anything, I went on.

A Warm Spring Evening

The dead dance and sing in a room near us.
We cannot see them because our lives are too busy;
that is, unless our loves lie in wreckage around us.
Then when the one companion left
is the photograph of the woman who left us,
they come softly, from their room to ours,
breathing with a soft quickness, from the dancing.
Only those who suffered as we do come,
and can come tenderly, and touch,
with their dead, beautiful hands, our shoulders,
like plum blossoms falling, like the wind
not quite stirring on these May nights,
to comfort us, to be our only real friends.
Their eyes regard us calmly, and with knowledge.
There is a stillness when the dead stop singing.
There is a beauty that we know who are in pain.
To be alone with the dead is to let our heart's wounds
be stanched, if only for a moment. Do not
be at peace, they mouth, their eyes now anxious.
Live, they insist, live in your time.

Notes

Part 1 was occasioned by living the better part of the year on the Greek island of Paros, in the Cyclades.

"Planet X" refers to the discovery of Pluto, by Clyde Tombaugh, in January, 1930.

Andiparos, in the poem of the same name, is a small island to the west of Paros. It is chiefly noted for its cave, which Lord Byron visited and in which he wrote his name.

The Alto Rhapsody is by Brahms.